Her Words of Wisdom

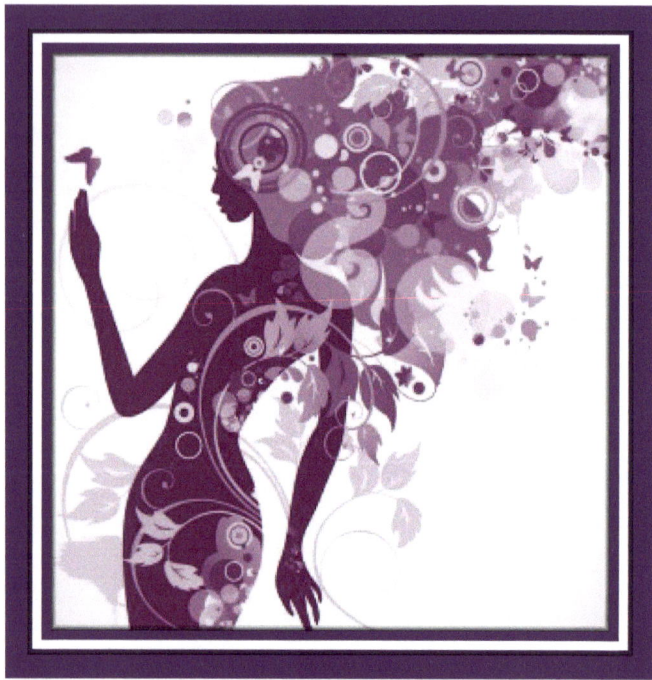

for

Kings & Queens

Her Words

of

Wisdom

Rekita Nelson

EPIPHANY ENCOUNTER
www.epiphanyencounter.com

Acknowledgements
Thank You

I'd first like to thank my Heavenly Father in creating this beautiful gift within and giving me the opportunity to share it with others. Heavenly Father, it was your hands that have provided and cared for me every step of the way. I'd like to thank you for wiping every tear from my eye, cheering me on when I doubted who I was in and through you, and for keeping a beautiful smile upon my face. My heart loves you more than you could ever know and I pray that this book **"Her Words of Wisdom,"** will reach and touch your people in ways they've never expected. I dedicate this book to You and to:

The Nelson & Latham Family

For this is who I am and this is who God has called me to be, And to all of my extended family and friends who have encouraged and supported me along the way.

Thank you,

Rekita

Contents

Her Words of Wisdom

About This Book

*The purpose of this book **"Her Words of Wisdom,"** allows you to have a moment of reflection on where you stand with your relationship with God, yourself, and others. This book is a workbook that guides you through the eyes of a mother who was called by God to raise her son as a king. The king precedes the throne and begins to seek insight, guidance, and understanding from his mother's words of wisdom. As you begin to navigate through the chapters you will see "tokens of wisdom" from the king's mother marked **"Her Words of Wisdom"**. In this book:*

* ❖ *Gain understanding on how to seek wisdom*
* ❖ *Gain understanding of the power of prayer and influence*
* ❖ *Gain understanding about listening to others*
* ❖ *Know your position and role within the kingdom of God*
* ❖ *Learn how to operate with authority*
* ❖ *Learn what it means to be equally yoked*
* ❖ *Understand who you are to God and to others*
* ❖ *Learn how to detect and overcome temptations*
* ❖ *Learn how to remain sober in the presence of God and others*
* ❖ *Gain understanding in societal injustice and oppression*
* ❖ *Know your value and your worth to God, yourself, and others*
* ❖ *Learn to walk with integrity and gain respect for yourself and from others*

Introduction: A Letter for You

Words from the Heart

Thank you for supporting this book. This book was created from my own personal devotion on the readings and teachings of King Lemuel's mother in the book of Proverbs within the Bible. I briefly paint a picture of the way the story would possibly unfold through the eyes of King Lemuel's mother. King Lemuel is now the king and his mother gently gives him the advice that he needs as he continues on learning his role and his position as a king. As you read these chapters, think about where you are on your journey with God, think about the position in which you are in, and how much of an influence you are to the body of Christ. As you read these chapters, allow the words to penetrate your heart and mind as you are gently reminded that you too are royalty. Remember, that you are fearfully and wonderfully made in the image of God. Understand that no matter where you are, whether within the palace walls or beyond the palace walls; you have the power to make a difference within the lives of those who are around you. What matters the most, is not your position but your level of influence that you have at home and within your community. I hope that this empowers you and challenges you for the better. I look forward to sharing more insight with you in the near future.

Your Sister in Christ,

Rekita

Her Words of Wisdom

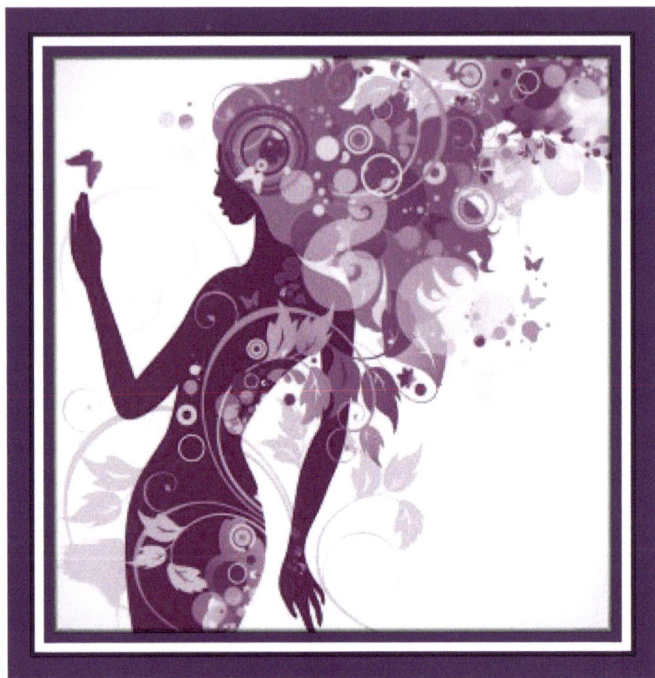

Let's Begin

A MOTHER'S PRAYER

The Birth of a King

There is nothing greater and more powerful than the power of a mother's prayers. A mother's petition goes before the throne of grace and God's ears and heart are turned towards her prayers. God proceeds to put things in place and He begins to align people, places, and things on the behalf of a mother who is praying for her son who is not yet here within the earth. As God begins to fashion him, in her womb one stitch at a time, making sure with every heart beat that he is fearfully and wonderfully made; we are able to see God's attentiveness to details. He is careful at how the child is fashioned for this is not just any ordinary child this is a child who is a result of prayer. This child is a result of what God can do in and through the lives of those who truly do love and believe in Him. As the story unfolds, the cries and the birth of a newborn son have arrived within the earth's realm. "He shall be called Lemuel, a king he shall forever be".

DAY 1

Are You Fit To Be A King?

The sayings of King Lemuel –
an inspired utterance his mother taught him. *–Proverbs 31:1*

A mother's love is indescribable. In fact, if you are blessed with having a mother you will understand that her love for you is irreplaceable. Now granted, not everyone has had the privilege of having a mother in their lives. Some mothers have abandoned their children, some are addicted to drugs, some maybe behind bars within the judicial system, and others have had their mothers go on to be with their ancestors. In this scenario, King Lemuel has been inspired by the words that his mother has taught him since he was a child. He sits high on the throne with the responsibilities of a king and now he is left to be a ruler within the land. Although, the book of Proverbs gives clear instructions from fathers to their sons, this particular chapter within the book of Proverbs is very significant in the role and influence of a mother and her instructions to her son. There are a few things that we could say about King Lemuel concerning this first verse. We can make the assumptions that King Lemuel is:

(1.) **In a position of authority** and needs some help in making decisions that are appropriate for his role and understanding his position.

(2.) **His mother remains an influential person** within his life. Her words meant so much to King Lemuel that he was willing to listen to *"Her Words of Wisdom,"* in order to be the best king that he could be.

(3.) King Lemuel **was a great listener.** He gained understanding on how to take what his mother taught him and apply it to where he needed.

(4.) **He understood who he was** in that he was not a product of himself but that he was a product of his mother. He could take her teachings and use them as his very own.

King Lemuel now sits on the throne and needs instructions. He begins to recognize that he needs guidance for his position. He understands his role as the future king but he doesn't grasp the fullness of leadership. He begins to seek advice when he doesn't understand. He recognizes that there will be times when he simply does not know which direction to go. The king's mother knew that her son would need her guidance. She knew that he was young and that using his own judgments would not get him very far in his role as king. Her motherly touch, love, and support were needed to run the kingdom. There is a popular saying that states, "Behind every good man there's a good woman". Being a mother, she would say as a token of *"Her Words of Wisdom,"* that if you are a woman and you have a man (son, brother, husband, nephew, etc.) in your life you have the opportunity to pour into who they are and to be an investor in who they will become.

As a woman your role has an impact on the developing and grooming of a young man. Men, it is wise to respect and honor the role in which a woman plays in your life. It doesn't matter if you agree to what she does or what she has done to you. Work at respecting the wonderful person she has helped in making you to be. Take the time to better understand your role as a king. Understand who you are in the earth and know that you have the power and authority to rule and reign over your own life. Understand and know who you are in and through Christ. This will allow you to carry a good name for yourself and be respected by others around you. King Lemuel understood that his reputation was of importance. He took the time to take in the instructions and advice of his mother so that he would not make a fool of his name or his family name. King Lemuel understood who he was and who he was going to be. He understood that in order for him to be successful as a king he was going to have to change his own mindset and adhere to the mindset of his mother. He knew that his mother would never steer him in the wrong direction which is why he sought her council.

A Moment of Reflection:

Think about the women who have influenced your life. Think about how they have influenced you and shaped you into the person that God has called you to be.

1.) Who is the woman in your life who has influenced you the most to be who you are today?

_____

_____

_____

2.) How does this woman contribute to where you are now and where you're going?

_____

_____

_____

3.) If you have struggles with a woman in your life what is the cause?

_____

_____

_____

4.) How can you work towards respecting the woman who is in your life and influencing you?

_____

_____

_____

5.) What are some of the ways that you can show the woman in your life your appreciation and gratitude for making you the man that you are today?

_____

_____

_____

DAY 2

The Power of Prayer

Listen, my son! Listen, son of my womb!
Listen, my son, the answer to my prayers! –Proverbs 31:2

Any woman who has ever had the privilege to be pregnant with child understands the overwhelming joy that it bears. Just to know that a living being that is so precious can be inside of you is a bond that cannot be explained but only experienced. King Lemuel's mother was a woman with an influential voice. She knew how powerful her voice was to King Lemuel from the time he was in her womb. She carried him for nine months full term and the bond in which they shared was enough to get his undivided attention when spoken too. She not only was able to influence King Lemuel to turn to her voice but she knew how to get King Lemuel's attention when he needed it most. Not only was she able to get the attention of her son but she was a woman who was able to receive God's undivided attention. Receiving His undivided attention shows you the power of her prayers.

Oh, the power of a praying woman who can shift the heart of God. A woman's voice is so powerful that it knocks at the door to our Heavenly Father's heart. God hears us when we pray. King Lemuel's mother made it a point to tell King Lemuel that you are a product of my prayers. You are not just a child that was born into this earth. You are a child that has destiny and purpose. You came to the earth from God. He planted you in my womb that you may grow into the king that He has called you to be. You are fearfully and wonderfully made. King Lemuel's mother didn't just understand the process in which she had to go through in order to deliver her blessing but she knew that God had answered her prayers just for her as she believed in Him.

King Lemuel's mother was a woman with gentle words and a woman of faith. She had to trust that God would answer her prayers even though she could not see God physically. She had to do what a lot of us women and men struggle with today. She had to step out on faith. She had to believe in the God in whom she serves. She had to trust that God would open her womb and bare her a son. She didn't just pray for a son but she prayed for a son that would listen to her words and to her teachings. She knew that her son may grow up with pride and arrogance from being in the lineage of kings; so her prayers, had to be with specific details that would allow God to give her the child that would be suitable to carry on the family name.

How important it is for us women to pray over the men who are in our lives. We are to ask God to place a special hedge fence of protection around the men in whom we love and care for. We should pray that God shapes and molds them into the men that God has called them to be within the earth. Women are to bring their prayers and petitions, before the throne of grace, with expectation that God is going to do just what we asked Him for. Men, you ought to listen to a woman, when she prays for you or over you for she is the gateway to your own prayer life. A woman has the power to touch God's heart in ways that are unexplainable. Learning how to touch the heart of God and how to chasten after God's own heart will bring you to a road of many blessings in your life.

A Moment of Reflection:

Consider your prayer life. Ask yourself where you are in your relationship with God. Think about, if you were to call on His name now, would you have the power to get God's undivided attention.

1.) How often do you pray within a day?

_____

_____

_____

2.) What are some things that you could do differently when you pray?

_____

_____

_____

3.) What do you pray for concerning your children?

_____

_____

_____

4.) How are you investing in your children's development and self-esteem?

_____

_____

_____

5.) Where do you stand with your faith in God?

_____

_____

_____

Her Words of Wisdom

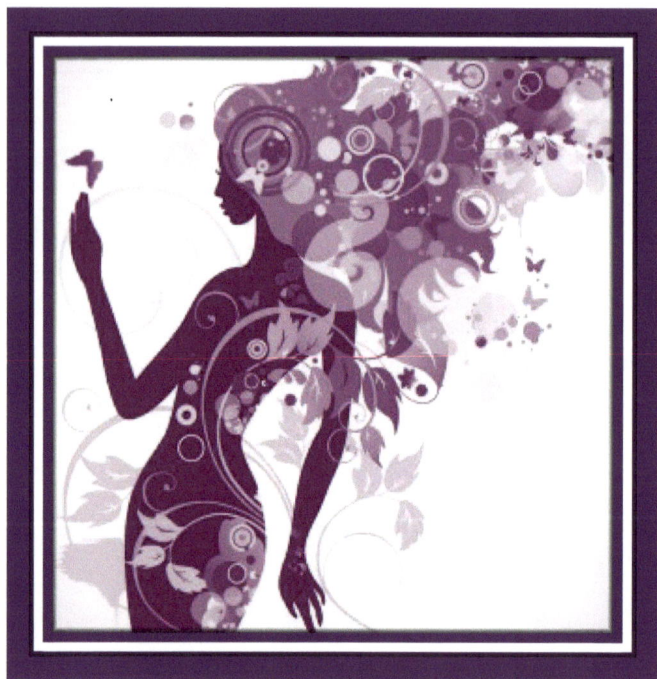

Prayer Changes Things

WORDS OF WISDOM

Fighting Temptations

*King Lemuel, would soon grow up to be a man, a man with questions that are truly meant for a father to answer. Instead, King Lemuel's mother begins to give him instructions, concerning fighting temptations that could lead him down a pathway of destruction. She begins to instruct him on what to look out for and why. She knows that she can no longer control the things in which he does; for he is a young man, who is more than capable of making his own decisions. She no longer can tell him which way to go and which way not to go as she did when he was just a young child. She recognizes that her son is growing into a man and that he is seeking words of wisdom and guidance from those around him. Her heart's desire is that he will find the right influential people who can set his feet on the right path. As she begins to instruct him with **"Her Words of Wisdom,"** she begins to pray that his heart and ears are listening to the echoes of her voice.*

Her Words of Wisdom

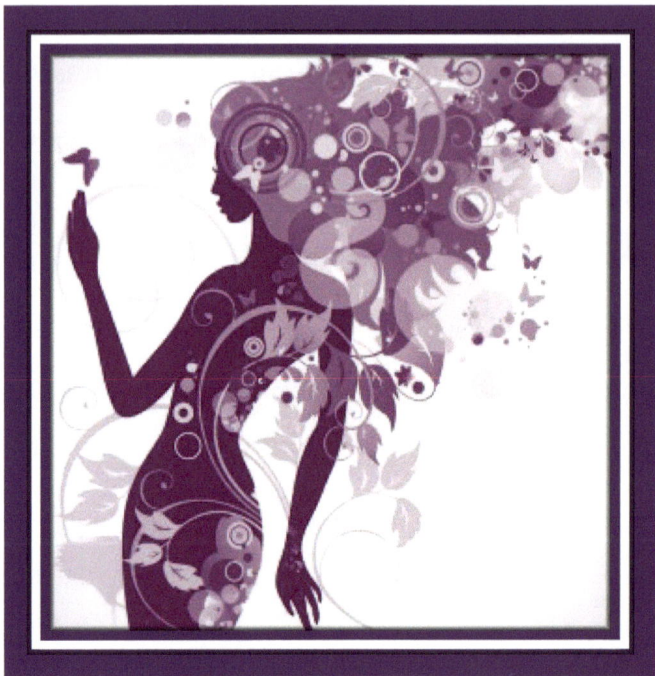

A Better Version of You

DAY 3

A King's Strength

Do not spend your strength[a] on women,
your vigor on those who ruin kings. –Proverbs 31:3

Men, you are so strong and courageous; not because of your abs, triceps, and biceps, but because you are a man who is created in the image of God Himself. Although, you are a man your strength lies within your authority. Authority is not to be used or abused. It is not made to hurt or harm others. Authority is made to rule and reign over a kingdom. You are the king that God has called you to be, just like King Lemuel. He was created in the image of God; and especially, crafted to perfection at the request and power of his own mother's prayers.

Men, you are to rule and reign within your homes. Sometimes, ruling and reigning means that you are willing to bow down to authority too. In order to be a great king, you must first know and understand what a great king prior to you did and how. As a token of *"Her Words of Wisdom,"* it is wise not to overstep your boundaries but to operate with a spirit of excellence when using your authority. There may be some instances, when you don't know how to be a king because you don't have the proper teachings. Sometimes, you don't know how to be a king because you don't have someone to show you or to lead you by example. A wise king heeds to the instructions of his mother (or authority), like King Lemuel did. God has blessed you with King Lemuel and his mother; so that you may understand and know, the way you are to rule and reign in your home as a king with authority. This does not give you permission to be controlling, but to be in control of your space and receive the respect that you desire to obtain.

Now let's receive a token of *"Her Words of Wisdom,"* from this third verse.

Her words would echo, to be careful in getting too concerned about what you don't have, but begin to count your blessings for everything that you do have. In this scenario, King Lemuel's mother did not want him to spend all of his strength and energy on women who didn't mean him any good. Men, if you are in a relationship and you do not have a positive woman who is shaping you and molding you into the man that God has called you to be, then chances are that may not be the woman for you. The Bible often times talks about being "unequally yoked" (2 Corinthians 6:14), that doesn't just mean in the aspect of unbelievers or even marriage. You have to be "equally yoked" in a number of things in your life; otherwise, you will spend your strength and energy on things that are not of importance. Being "equally yoked," brings forth balance and harmony, while causing you to make progression instead of digressing.

Men, it is wise to surround yourself with other men, who are able to help you grow and be the man that God has called you to be. Surrounding yourself with positive influences, who can take you to another level and a different dimension in and through God, is where you should consider being, according to King Lemuel's mother. If you waste your vigor on things that are outside of the will of God, it may cause you to spiral downhill rather than climb uphill. King Lemuel's mother gently tells her son, that surrounding yourself with individuals who can destroy your call, your purpose, and your family name is simply not the right path to take. She warns him out of love to be careful at whom you allow to pour into your heart, mind, and spirit. She gently shows King Lemuel his value and his worth as a king.

A Moment of Reflection:

Today, think about where you stand in your strength. Decide to make God your strength when you feel weak. Think about how King Lemuel might have felt being raised and told what to do by a woman, his mother.

1.) Who is in your space that could possibly cause you to digress instead of progress?

_____

_____

_____

2.) What does "unequally yoked" mean to you and how does this affect your life now? What can you change to become "equally yoked" and how?

_____

_____

_____

3.) Do you feel like you have authority over your life, if not, how can you change it?

_____

_____

_____

4.) Do you have a positive mentor in your life that is shaping and molding you into what God has called you to be?

_____

_____

_____

5.) What are you spending your strength and energy on? Is it causing you to digress or make progress?

_____

_____

_____

DAY 4

King's and Queen's Remain Sober

It is not for kings, Lemuel –
it is not for kings to drink wine,
not for rulers to crave beer... –Proverbs 31:4

This verse is a very sensitive topic when you consider substance abuse. Being on prescription drugs or over the counter medications, if not careful, may cause many different side effects and possibly cause an addiction; which, usually states so on the pamphlet or label that is given alongside of a drug. Drinking, on the other hand, may cause a little more damage over time. If not careful, drinking can possibly turn into a disease that can do damage to your overall health and well-being. King Lemuel's mother understood the importance of what it meant to not become drunk, due to the side effects. Blurred vision, slurred speech, and lack of clarity were not what many would have considered to be suitable for a king. King Lemuel's mother understood his position within the kingdom; that his being impaired could cause more damage than good.

King Lemuel's mother, knew that the role of a king would mean, that he would have to remain fair and give sound judgment where needed. She understood that to have one drink, would turn into several drinks, which would later turn into a craving. She wanted the best for her son. She knew that a clear mind and a sound conscious would allow him to make decisions that would heal their land. King Lemuel's mother wanted to make sure that her son was conducting himself in a professional manner, at all times. She didn't want him to dress inappropriately on account of being so drunk that he couldn't distinguish his shoe from his crown. Being drunk and reigning would have been considered unacceptable behavior in the king's position.

Men and women can both have cravings for alcoholic beverages, if not careful. It actually is not about being careful, as much as, it is about not drinking at all while on the assignment. While, society and cultures may consider drinking to be socially acceptable; it is important, that kings and queens recognize that too much drinking can cause you to be dethroned. Drinking, is not just bad for better judgment but it can bring harm and danger to those who are close to you. If not careful, it may cause tragic accidents and more. Taking the time, to have a clear conscious and to operate with fairness not only will give you respect but honor. Being a king or queen is not just for those who are in authority or in position; but being a king or queen, means you understand the importance of what it means to be a leader. You understand what it means to lead by example. You understand that others are watching your every move. They are inspired by you when you have a clear mind and can make wise decisions where needed.

King Lemuel's mother understood the power of prayer. She understood what it took to be in the presence of the Lord. She knew that drinking would not be an option when going before God to ask for a son. She knew that God would not be able to hear her or turn towards her if she came before God in an inappropriate manner, considering her own position as a queen. Raising a son, while she was drunk, would not have been an option for her when raising a king. She understood the importance of what it means to lead by example; due to her son, being old enough to watch her every move. Her son was learning the lineage of royalty. In order for him to carry on the mantle, as his mother, she had to grace her own actions with the actions and things of God. If she wanted her son, to follow in the ways of her God, then she understood that it would be important if she teaches King Lemuel by example.

A Moment of Reflection:

As a woman or man of God, think or consider your own lifestyle and how you are living. Remember, that God loves everyone and that we are all sinners who have fallen short of His glory. (If you are having troubles with alcohol or drug addiction, be sure to seek professional help to receive the support that you need.)

1.) What are ways that you can challenge yourself from drinking socially to not drinking at all?

_____

_____

_____

2.) Has alcohol or drugs affected your lifestyle? If so, what are you doing to get the professional help and support that you need?

_____

_____

_____

3.) One of the spiritual side effects is not being able to hear from God, how does that make you feel within? What can you do to change how you feel and draw closer to God again?

_____

_____

_____

4.) Do you feel that it is important for a king or queen to remain sober? Why or why not?

_____

_____

_____

5.) Is this the lifestyle that you desire to live? If not, how are you going to change it and how are you going to maintain the change?

_____

_____

_____

DAY 5

Justice or Else

...lest they drink and forget what has been decreed,
and deprive all the oppressed of their rights. –Proverbs 31:5

We've established that King Lemuel's mother felt that drinking can cause some form of impairment in one's judgment. We've also established that King Lemuel's mother was a woman with a voice, a woman of prayer, a woman of faith, and a woman of integrity. She believed that carrying yourself appropriately in the public's eye and behind closed doors was of importance. Her heart, was not only, wrapped up in the things of God; but, her heart was wrapped up in the things concerning her son. For King Lemuel's mother, making sure that her son was carrying on the family name with dignity and respect mattered to her.

King Lemuel's mother was a woman who believed in education. She wanted him to have the best education and the best teachers who could teach him the laws of the land. Who would be greater than herself, considering that God declared, "These commandments that I give you today are to be on your hearts. Impress them on your children. Talk about them when you sit at home and when you walk along the road, when you lie down and when you get up" (Deuteronomy 6:6-7, NIV). His mother's heart was open to the commandments of God. Not only, did she want to impress them onto King Lemuel's heart, but she wanted to make sure that he understood the importance of the law and decree. It was a part of his inheritance. She understood that sitting down with him and teaching him would prepare him to be the king that God had called him to be. Her heart's desire was to make sure he was wrapped up in the heart of God just as much as she was. Yet, she knew and understood that it would take teaching her son what was right and what was wrong, according to the laws of the land.

Like most women, we appreciate it when our men both young and old remember us. We appreciate when the men in our lives take the time not to forget the things that matter most to our hearts. Women tend to cherish these things in their hearts and it makes us feel really special within. Men, one of the most important things you could ever do when it comes to a woman, is remember the things that matter most to her heart. If you can just keep those things in mind and work really hard at not forgetting, then it may get you a lot farther with what it is that you need and want from a woman. For instance, a woman's birthday, her favorite dessert, her favorite things to do, all of these things matter to a woman and can be to your advantage if you use it properly. Studying a woman can be one of the greatest things you could ever do. It doesn't matter if she is your grandmother, mother, wife, girlfriend, daughter, or sister, knowing what she really likes and not forgetting could simply brighten up her day and become a blessing to her. King Lemuel's mother understood this. She wanted to make sure that drinking would not let him forget who he was and who he was called to be as a king.

Oppression can be a very sensitive topic in today's society. It is sensitive, in the fact that, it is not grasped and understood properly by those who have never experienced oppression. It is important, that one studies and learns different cultures and backgrounds of others who have been through oppression; so that, your hearts are sensitive to the needs of those who are and have been oppressed. King Lemuel's mother understood that if she taught her son the laws of the land, that none of it mattered if he could not operate with integrity. If he could not carry his duties out as king, then she knew that it would not help or bless anyone else. She made it her business to teach King Lemuel that drinking is not an option for him, while handling the oppressed. It was not an option for him due to the role and leadership position that he held. She wanted King Lemuel to make sure that he was aware of his surroundings, could quickly find solutions to problems, and was capable of judging fairly and more. Her gentle words to King Lemuel, and token of *"Her Word of Wisdom,"* is to make sure that he understood the rights of those who were being oppressed; and that, he gives to them the appropriate measures of justice that is due to them. Her love for King Lemuel continued to flourish, as she continues, to shape him and mold him into the man and king that God has called him to be.

A Moment of Reflection:

Consider why it was so important for King Lemuel to stay away from drinking. Think about how drunkenness could impair his judgment as king and bring more harm than good to the land.

1.) Do you remember the things that are important to those who matter to you most?

_____

_____

_____

2.) Are you being fair and just in the position that you hold at home, work, or in school?

_____

_____

_____

3.) Do you study the Bible as a means to refresh and educate yourself on the laws that God created for his people?

_____

_____

_____

4.) Have you taught your children what is right and wrong so that they will walk with integrity? How will this better them as well as you?

_____

_____

_____

5.) What cultures have you studied that may have gone through oppression? What did you learn?

_____

_____

_____

Her Words of Wisdom

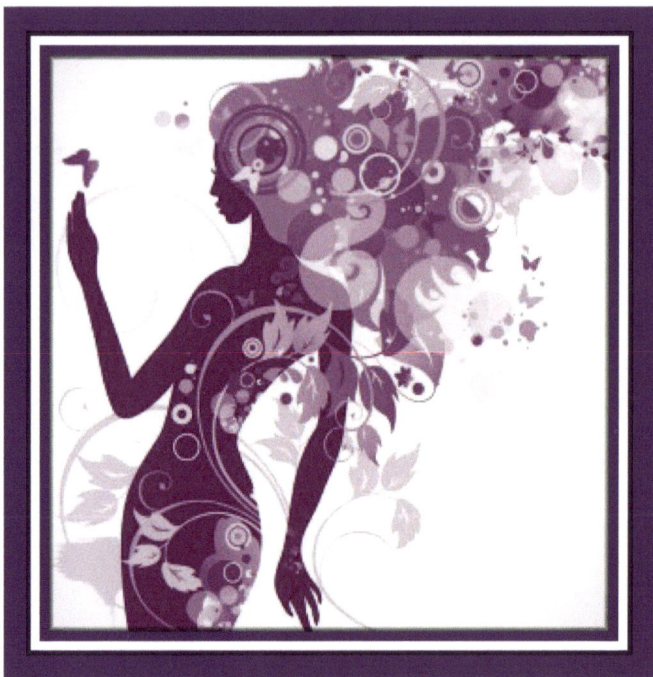

You Shall Live

DAY 6

You Shall Not Perish

Let beer be for those who are perishing,
wine for those who are in anguish! *--Proverbs 31:6*

King Lemuel's mother goes even further into details with him on the importance of not drinking. She not only takes a moment to build him up in his manhood, but she also allows him to see that it is important that he learns how to maintain a level head. King Lemuel was conceived and carried by his mother for nine months. She refrained from putting any drink to her lips while carrying her son. Instructions were gently whispered to her through the relationship that she shared with God and possibly with the mid-wives of her time. She continued on to raise her son with the same mentality concerning drinking. She did not want him to drink because she knew the effects it could have on her son. Drunkenness can lead to becoming violent and belligerent and that was not the character or the nature of a king. She worked hard at teaching him about character and how his character determines the reputation in which he would carry. She taught him the importance of his family name and how he should carry himself at all times with good character and integrity.

King Lemuel's mother shows her strength as a mother as she begins to teach him who he is. Raising a young man who is fit to be a king would be a challenge; but she was determined, to make sure that he was all that he was called to be. She began to tell him and encourage him as a king, not as her son alone. She began from the womb to build up his self-esteem and make him aware of the perils of this world. She let him know that he would not perish in this world as he takes up his rightful place as king. She teaches him to not be intimidated by life itself but to stand firm and take up his rightful position without fear.

She explains to him the lineage of his royalty and that perishing is not an option for him as a king. She teaches him his value and his worth, not only, to the kingdom but to himself. She takes the time to explain that being drunk will not help him to see or understand who he is as a man or as a king. She goes further to instruct him that if he is searching for his manhood and trying to find out who he is, then drinking is not the appropriate way to do so. King Lemuel's mother understands that she is a woman who can only teach her son so much about being a man. She knows that surrounding her son with his father, the proper mentors, and leaders who they both could trust is of importance.

Not only, did she desire to teach King Lemuel his value and his worth, she wanted to explain to him that not every day is going to be a good day. There will be some good days and there will be some bad days; but when those days arise, it is not for him to perish away and become angry at the very things he possibly cannot control. She understood that it does not get you anywhere when you begin to think out of your emotions as a king, versus logically. They both work hand in hand; but as her son, she wanted him to know that he has to be able to maintain a level head in order to make the appropriate decisions. King Lemuel's mother took her son's role very seriously. She knew what would tempt and try him, as he was embarking upon becoming a man, who is about to take a major leadership position. She understood the male ego and knew that pride could get in the way, if he was not careful. She shaped and molded him until he understood that anger was not the way to have victory; but, that it was the very thing that could destroy everything that he worked hard to build and maintain.

A Moment of Reflection:

Think about King Lemuel and what it took to be a king at such a young age. Think about King Lemuel and what would have happened within the kingdom if he didn't control his anger.

1.) What are ways that you can keep your family name from perishing?

_____

_____

_____

2.) What are ways you could release the anger that you may feel inside without being violent or belligerent?

_____

_____

_____

3.) How have the perils of this world affected you and how you view your own value and self-worth?

_____

_____

_____

4.) As a woman how do you see yourself being effective in the men who you are connected to? As a man how do you see yourself being effective in the women you are connected to?

_____

_____

_____

5.) What temptations do you face? How can you avoid these temptations?

_____

_____

_____

DAY 7

Beyond The Palace Walls

Let them drink and forget their poverty
and remember their misery no more. –Proverbs 31:7

King Lemuel's mother was a very experienced woman. She seemed to have known, that the grass wasn't greener on the other side of the palace walls. She knew what was out there and what her Lemuel would soon have to face. She prepared him for what he would face as a king. She tried to protect him from too much to drink, due to the fact that, she worked too hard to get to where she was. She wasn't going to allow her son to ruin everything that she had built, in order to make it. She wanted the best for her son and she worked hard at giving it to him and providing it for him. Even if it meant, that she had to do things like the queen she was called to be. She had to have character and skills, so that she could pass these things down to her son. She wanted her Lemuel to know that life hasn't always been easy; but, that if he put his faith in God and followed after her own teachings that he would never go astray. She had a true heart of a mother and she wanted him to know, that everything that she did and all of what she had been through, was so that he wouldn't have to take the same narrow path that she did.

Poverty, had stricken the land outside of the palace walls. Her son, never being exposed to this, now has to face the realities of what lies outside of the palace walls. He now has to see and understand that he is privileged. He has to now see, that not everyone has the same advantages or opportunities that he has. King Lemuel had not yet been exposed, to what was outside of the city walls; other than, from the stories he heard within the walls of the palace. He understood what it meant to drink, for there were many feast within the palace. What King Lemuel had to learn and understand is how a drink would no longer be for pleasure on account of celebration and fellowship; but how, it would be a drink to numb the pains of one's reality. The reality was that God's people were being oppressed; and there was one person, who had the power to change the written laws with his signet ring. King Lemuel had to face the realities, of whether or not, he was going to rule fairly and just or let the laws continue to be the same as God's people remain oppressed.

King Lemuel's mother wanted in her heart to protect her son, like any mother, from the perils of this world. She knew that she could either protect him and he rebel; he can find out on his own; or she could protect him in a different manner by teaching it to him and giving him the option to make a wise decision to rule fairly. She chose to teach her Lemuel things that she knew would cross his path and that he would need better insight and more clarity, poverty being one of them. Never, had King Lemuel been exposed, to what was outside of the palace walls. He never had to face anything, other than, what was already placed and set before him. He had to learn about poverty and what it meant to be without. He had to learn how to relate and have a better understanding. He had to be exposed to these challenges that would arise amongst God's people; which means, he had to be ready and prepared to judge effectively and accordingly.

A Moment of Reflection:

King Lemuel's mother loved him very much. She worked hard at providing for him the nice things that others outside of the palace walls didn't have. It sometimes meant that she had to sacrifice and follow the ways of a queen, in order to fulfill her own duties.

1.) What are some of the positive attributes that you see in King Lemuel's mother that you see within you?

_____

_____

_____

2.) Do you feel that King Lemuel's mother was right or wrong for exposing her son to the realities outside of the palace wall? Why?

_____

_____

_____

3.) Do you feel that King Lemuel was in position to handle being a king to God's people? Why?

_____

_____

_____

4.) How often do you find yourself thinking that the grass is greener on the other side? What causes you to believe so?

_____

_____

_____

5.) Do you believe that there are benefits in exposure? Why or Why not?

_____

_____

_____

Her Words of Wisdom

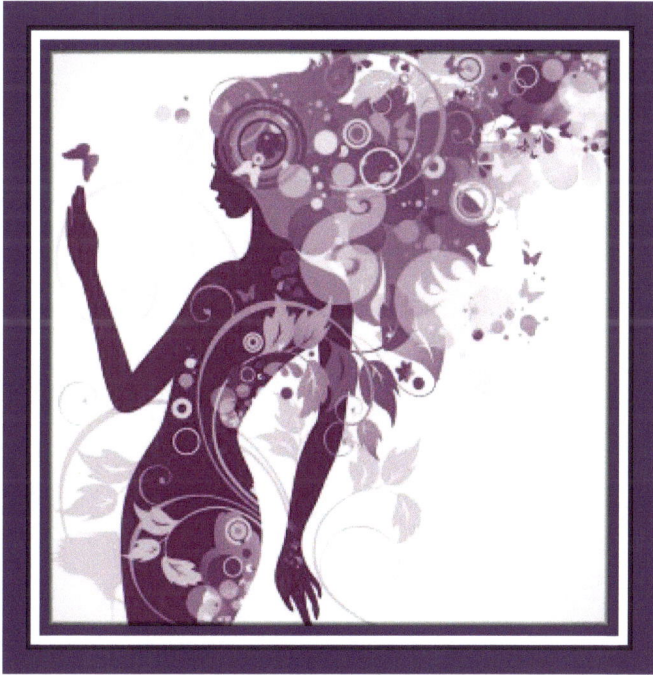

Think About Others

HE REIGNS

A Voice in the Land

Princes usually take up their reigns as king by succession. King Lemuel's story isn't very definite of how he preceded the throne. All we know is that, he had a praying mother in his corner that was not hesitant to knock on the gates of heaven for the son she loved. King Lemuel, still young but mature enough to seek the advice of his elders, begins to learn that there is more to his position than just being king. He begins to explore his new position and recognizes that he has to speak up. He has to be willing to learn public speaking skills, in which, he is not prepared to do so. Although, he may not feel prepared, he still had a mother who prayed a prayer many years ago; and now, it is time for King Lemuel to activate the public speaking skills that God has placed within him. How he would do it would be interesting to explore and who he would do it on would be even more interesting. King Lemuel now is going to actually have to stand up for people who are less privileged than he is. He is going to have to learn what it means to relate to a people who were considered beneath his status quo. He will now have to advocate for the oppressed and be a voice in the land.

DAY 8

Your Voice Has Power

Speak up for those who cannot speak for themselves,
for the rights of all who are destitute. –Proverbs 31:8

King Lemuel's mother understood her community. She understood what was outside of the palace walls. She also understood who was inside of the palace walls with the power to make the decisions for those who were living on the outside. Her son was the next in line to take on the torch, to take up the mantle; and now, it was his turn to lead God's people to where God wanted and needed for them to be. King Lemuel, young and unsure of what he was up against, asked his mother for guidance and direction. What should I do? How should I handle this situation? What about when this happens? These were all of the many questions and challenges that the king was up against. King Lemuel's mother, a woman of such wisdom, spoke to him with such gentleness.

King Lemuel's mother stretched her son's ability to have a clear and precise understanding of what it meant to be a king, but to give sound judgment. Being a king was more than just being a ruler over many. Being a king was more than wearing royal robes and the finest bejeweled crown. Being a king meant carrying on the family name with dignity, respect, honor, and fairness. Being a king of integrity would set the tone for the level of respect he would receive from the people. King Lemuel faced many people who were mistreated on account of oppression. His mother's main concern was for him to be a king who ruled and judged with justice, a king who stood up for those who could not stand up for themselves, and a king who stepped in to help those who had the bare minimum to survive.

She taught her Lemuel to speak for God's people and to make sure that they received what was needed to survive. In their case, it was not about those who were already well off and who had, but it was about those who were less fortunate, those who were classified as poor, lower income, poverty-stricken, impoverished individuals who just could not do for themselves. She wanted her son to have a heart that could not only hear from God, but hear her voice, as well as, hear the silent cries of God's people. She raised him to be a wise king who could make decisions the right way. She understood that the laws of the land would hurt people and she understood who had the power to release the spirit of oppression from off of God's people.

King Lemuel and his mother had the power to do what others could not do for themselves. She wanted to make sure that he was using his power justly. She was raising a young man who would stand before many. She wanted him to carry his scepter with sovereignty. In doing so, it was important for King Lemuel to study the land. It was important for him to understand how prosperous he was in comparison to others. It was important for him to see that his wealth and riches did not define him, but the integrity of his heart did. It defined him into the king that others would perceive him as. It showed that he was a man after God's own heart and a man who was for God's people.

A Moment of Reflection:

King Lemuel ruled his kingdom with just power and a voice to make a difference within the land. He was able to win the hearts of God's people by making a way for God's people.

1.) How are you making a difference within your community?

_____

_____

_____

2.) How do you treat others who are less fortunate than you? Do you speak up for them?

_____

_____

_____

3.) What are some of the things that you could do differently to help someone who is less fortunate than you are?

_____

_____

_____

4.) What are some signs of oppression that are going on within your community? What can you do to help change it?

_____

_____

_____

5.) What are ways that you can make sound judgment and practice fairness in your own life?

_____

_____

_____

DAY 9

It's About God's People

Speak up and judge fairly;
defend the rights of the poor and needy. –Proverbs 31:9

As the realities of his position gained more attention, King Lemuel was left to not only be a king, but he was left to be a judge. He was left to judge the people and handle their situations that they could not handle on their own. He was in position to take charge and to take the lead. He didn't have anyone who could teach him what it meant to be a king. He didn't have anyone who left him a handbook or a manual. All he had was his faith and trust in God and the powerful voice of His mother who raised him to be all of what He was called to be. King Lemuel didn't always know exactly where to begin. He didn't have everything learned, in fact majority of what he had to face was a "learn as you go" type of experience. Sometimes he would get it right and other times he had to try again the next time. His focus no longer could be on whether or not he had his position down and intact, but rather on whether or not God's people were taken care of fairly.

As the words echoes, in the heart of King Lemuel, he begins to see that those who are not being treated fairly must be judged fairly. He begins to advocate on the behalf of the oppressed. He begins to stand up for those who can't stand up and defend themselves. He has explored beyond the palace walls; and, he recognizes that there is more to the stories of each individual person. He sees that they each didn't land in this position by accident. He sees that the laws of the land could be better written. He sees that the laws could be catered to the needs and the struggles of God's people. He sees that there is so much more that can be done and he recognizes that he has the power to change it. He may be young, but he has a voice that will be respected and that will be heard. He knows that he can withstand the legalistic matters; because, he too took a scholarly course while in training and knows what is right and wrong. He knows and can distinguish when others who are more privileged are trying to get over on those who are less privileged. King Lemuel can now take up his scepter and reign like the king that he is called to be. He now can determine the needs of God's people and work with them, as well as, alongside of them.

"King's Lemuel's mother did a fine job of raising that young man, "were the whispers beyond the palace walls. King Lemuel's mother wanted his name to be great within the earth. God heard her prayers when she prayed for him. He heard her prayers when he became King as well. He didn't know everything but his mother taught him everything she knew to keep him from being in trouble. She did everything that she could to keep him from being around the wrong people and being around the right influences. Her son could now rule the land with her being his private adviser. Her voice was all that he needed to get through those challenging days. Her touch was all he needed to know that everything is going to be just fine, even on those not so good days. She believed in her son more than anyone and she knew he was capable of getting the tasks at hand done, in the right way. She cheered him on, she challenged him, and she encouraged him. She continued to make a way out of no way for him until he was old enough to make a way out of no way for her. She raised him the best way she knew how and he turned out to be a fine king who ruled and reigned over the land.

A Moment of Reflection:

King Lemuel learned a lot of what he knew about being a king from his mother and her teachings. He understood that he was in position to do justly by God's people. He understood that he was not in position just for himself.

1.) How do you think King Lemuel handled his position considering that his mother was his main influential voice?

_____

_____

_____

2.) Who are the people or the voices in your life that help to influence you? Are they positive or negative influences?

_____

_____

_____

3.) What position are you in now and how does your position benefit those who are around you?

_____

_____

_____

4.) When challenges arise, how do you help those who may not feel their voice is being heard?

_____

_____

_____

5.) Do you believe that you make a difference in the lives of others? How?

_____

_____

_____

Final Words

*I hope that you have enjoyed your readings from **"Her Words of Wisdom."** I do appreciate your support on this book. Please feel free to follow me on the social media sites below. Please continue to keep me in your prayers as I allow God to do greater works in and through me daily. Allow me to take a brief moment to pray with you.*

Heavenly Father,
Cover my brother's and sister's, through Christ, in your wings as they meditate on the words that You have given me to share. I pray that the readings and the moments of reflections will change and transform their lives from day to day. Continue to bless each of them as you shape and mold them into the King's and/or Queen's you have called them to be. May your light shine in each of them. In Jesus name we pray. Amen.
Many Blessings,

Rekita Nelson

Please Like/Follow me on social media:

Instagram: @DANYALLE_83

Twitter: @DANYALLE_83

Facebook: www.facebook.com/epiphanyencounter

Images: Vector Graphics Abstract

Her Words of Wisdom

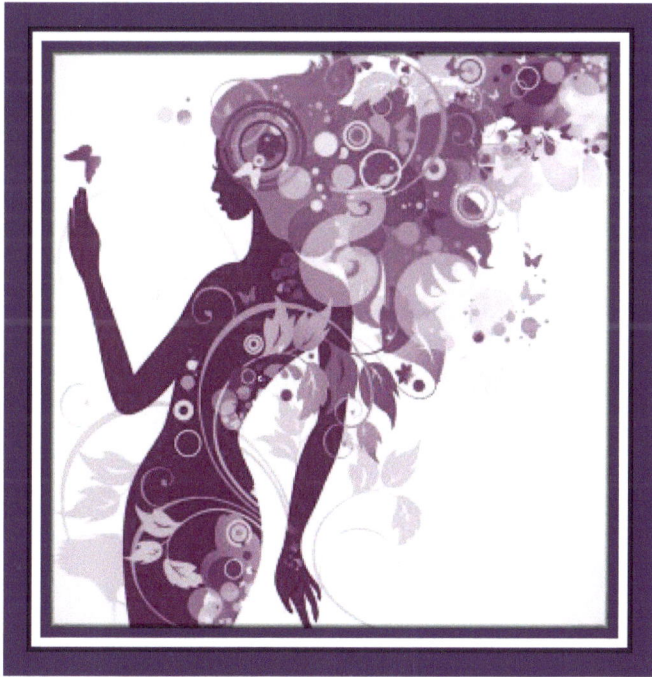

The End

www.ingramcontent.com/pod-product-compliance
Lightning Source LLC
Chambersburg PA
CBHW041802040426
42448CB00001B/11